Not All Who Are Lost Wander

poems by

Jonie McIntire

Finishing Line Press
Georgetown, Kentucky

Not All Who Are Lost Wander

ACKNOWLEDGMENTS

The author wishes to thank the publications in which some poems in this book
first appeared:

"Afterglow," *Broadway Bards First*, 2010.
"Love Is A Carcass," 2016 Hessler Street Fair Poetry Anthology, 2016.
"Week Night," *Toledo City Paper*, August-Issue 1-2015.

Publisher: Leah Maines

Editor: Christen Kincaid

Cover Art: Adrian Lime

Author Photo: Adrian Lime

Cover Design: Elizabeth Maines

Printed in the USA on acid-free paper.
Order online: www.finishinglinepress.com
also available on amazon.com

Author inquiries and mail orders:
Finishing Line Press
P. O. Box 1626
Georgetown, Kentucky 40324
U. S. A.

Table of Contents

*This book is dedicated to John Swaile
and the Almeda Street poets.*

Love Is a Carcass

A roasted grocery chicken,
purchased as dinner
with a coupon about to expire,
fills the car in steam.
The smell seeps in before
the front door is fully open
and the children run up,
eagerly hungry.

We barely make it to the table—
our savage fingers
dripping flesh into our mouths.
Our lips glisten smiles
and you walk in, laughing—
look at us!

We talk, cheeks full,
of the time with the fish
on the grill, whole
with his eyes and us
circling with forks.

Then another time with
snow forts, the second baby
coming home, and earlier,
to the first baby—

and all the while
both kids chime in with
memories they don't have
but heard. They are
wide-eyed and we have talked
back, long before the work
left and the bills
turned red,
before we two became
we four, back

to our audacious wedding,
only fifteen minutes long
with flies and hayrides,
and the Sharon Olds poem
and how we refused to explain
that moo shu pork
is a vow, that love is a carcass.

Our fingers are filthy
and we find rags
to wipe them off,
the four of us
rubbing our bellies,
placing bones in water
to make tomorrow's soup
from the juice.

The Day Begins

The woman wakes.
The dream is forgetting.
The left leg is cold.
The alarm is not yet ringing.
The floor is cold.
The hallway is dark.
The light is turned on.
The stairs are dusty.
The kitchen is dirty.
The dishwasher has clean dishes.
The bacon is frying.
The coffee is brewing.
The woman walks up the stairs.
She awakens the children and husband.
The woman walks down the stairs with the boy.
The dishes are set.
The juice is poured.
The breakfast is served.
The woman walks up the stairs.
The girl and the man are told
to wake-up.
The woman walks down the stairs.
The man and the girl walk down the stairs.
The day begins.

Inconclusive

In grade school,
they would test twice,
make her lift her shirt
so her back
was to the air,
her spine a chart
of correct or incorrect,
like a row
small circles penciled,
as if a key
would fit just over,
revealing where
each bone
should and should
not be.

When the two cars hit,
her pelvis crushed
into bucket seating.
Only bones were broken.
Plates and pins
pulled them together,
physical therapy
and six months
being careful
and she healed.
Though, the bones
don't line up
quite right.
Never will.

As they talked,
three hours and fourth date
barely begun,
he asked if she wanted
children, how many,
what names.
No. She'd never
even considered.
Her body,
barely twenty,
mapped poorly,
tests
inconclusive.

Queen Anne's Lace

Spread out
in a field,
a common thing
and wild,
just dainty enough
like something fine,
like linen,
pressed
for special occasions.

We run through the field,
dragging our
open hands,
pulling the
delicate flower tops
off until our fingers
stink of green
and our shoes
are no longer
white.

Aromatherapy

Place your nose
atop the baby's head.

Be sure
to close
your eyes.

The world does not exist.

Breathe
in.

Breathe again,
the little hairs
tickling your nose,
the warm head
soft, your lips
gentle.

Your mind clears
like mist
burned away
in the first rays
of light.

Ten and three and two and one

At seven years old,
he dreams in numbers.
The sound of them,
their gentle lines and curves.
He eats the concept of pi,
brushes his teeth
to repetition.

Pattern and sub pattern.

Ten Craisins,
three cashews,
two spinach leaves
and a Goldfish cracker.

These
mean something.

Now, just
ten and three and two and one
as a snack,
as we watch him
study each item,
arrange them
perhaps into something
random or stuck
ten and three and two and one
like a record
on a groove
unintended.

Or perhaps
later revealed,
a theorem
to be added
to the History of Numbers
hardback tucked
on the paper-strewn shelf
next to his bed.

Happiness is a climbing tree
inspired by Charles Schultz

The past two days have been hard in the way
we feel pain and hold it quiet,
but keep the children fed and gas in the car.
We rely on lists and the deadlines scratched
onto kitchen calendars in skipping pens.

A friend from college has died young and
you hold your breath every time
I mention looking for work.
Our minds are always on another
branch, snapping twigs.

You say no, McDonalds is not an option
and I agree. I see where you stand,
and remember a line about patchouli
in one of John Swaile's sestinas,
that her smell lingered long after she left.

You let out your breath and open your palm
flat and hot on my shoulder.
I cover your hand in mine,
ask what should we have for dinner
and stay close, always ready
to reach out when you grasp.

Weeknight

Just now ten at night
and I can sit,
drink a beer
while the dishes soak.

The children listen
in bed to radios
and books on disc,
the noise floating down
like mechanical whispers.

The stop sign
at the end of the street
has been removed,
deemed
unnecessary by the city,
so cars stream by,
like a constant
Dali river
our house is
tucked under.

This is as quiet
as it gets.

I want tv then! I want noise
and lights that live in one box,
where the fighting is a focus.
Where the bout is
already over and rerunning
in my tired shoulders,
in my aching arches.

But instead,
I write
something small.

And the cars quiet
and the clocks chorus
the radio whispers,
and in between stanzas,
my beer is so cold.

Goldfish

Still as a ribbon of orange
trapped in a glass paperweight,
he hovers in the center of the bowl,
a trail of feces
hanging down like a penis.

For three whole minutes now,
no movement and he faces
just to the left of me, as if
waiting,

as if asking
why am I still up
so late, the light on
and such a thin nightgown.

Corporate

In the parking lot,
you flip your visor up
to reveal a thin strip
of yourself, staring,
grey-haired and absent-minded,
back.

Business takes a breath,
from its teeth your thirties,
your forties hang like
shredded pork falling from corners.

Your eyes are quiet exhaustion.
Past your car,
a man and a woman walk,
telling a joke you've
heard before but liked.

And you open,
door wide, and call out—
wait, just a moment,
we'll walk in together.

Heart Attack
for Dave Hopson

It is possible that,
as your heart seized
and your last breaths
were escaping your body,
unexpectedly at the car showroom,
you having just walked
from the bus stop and still
catching your breath
from crossing so busy a street,

it is possible
that air escaped elsewhere
as well. Probable,
in fact, as we insisted
on El Camino for lunch
and lingered, talking
about the custom car mats
you would pick up
for your mother for
Christmas after work

and somehow we segued into
your absolute assurance
that your wife's claim
that you fart in your sleep
is false. She cannot possibly prove it.
Perhaps, there at the car dealership,
your body betrayed
your well-trained modesty.

But I'm sure nobody noticed
so your secret is safe with her.

Sin

As a child, I knew
sin was delicious and rare.
Only grandmas gave you
whole candy bars,
chocolate ice cream
right before bed, cola with
caffeine in it and cereals
they never ate but kept
in the cupboard just for you.
They made you promise
not to tell mom.

Sometimes they weren't grandma—
sometimes they were visiting aunts
and uncles, all hair and weird clothes,
booming voices with handbags and
spittle when they talk.
They would announce it,
flaunt indulgence to your parents,
daring them. Then they would watch
you as you ate, as if they could taste
joy through your fingers on the wrapper,
your studious discovery of each
melted bit until the wrapper
reflected better than mirrors.

But now, 10:30 am
Tuesday and I'm nearing forty,
I find change in a pocket
and thumb my nose
at the step-counters and diet-trackers
around me at work and I take
the elevator to a vending machine.
I return to my desk,
sit down solemnly, like
I'm lighting a holy hidden candle,
and I unwrap sweetness.

It's over too quickly now
and my mother
doesn't even ask.

Beets

Deep green with dark
red veins, scattered in a colander.
To warm the house,
she is roasting.
In one pan,
turkey from the Amish
who lost their son,
a bag of onions peeled
circle the bird, with
rosemary and oregano.
In the other pan, beets.
Just beets.
The deep rose staining
her fingerprints.
She pens a letter
to her daughter—the usual talk
of books and food and work.
Calling is useless.
Neither ever answers.
On the edges of the paper,
small fuchsia circles trace
what she's touched, where
she holds the paper still
so it won't slip away.
From the oven,
heat flows in waves circling
with January air
seeping in through thin walls,
and she sniffs the rosemary,
the copper smell of beets
bleeding slowly,
and pulls her sweater tighter,
turning the page
to write on its back.

Yellow Light

From the beginning,
our timing has been off

and the light turns yellow
just as we roll up

in the new car we've
already paid late twice,

you, correcting my grammar
from an argument

begun across town
and me, my palm flat

on the roof, watching the light
and mouthing "padiddle"

to keep us safe from red.

Where I Find Will

In the next to last pages of stacked legal pads.
In the center drawer of a 1000-pound metal desk.
In the folded white undershirts, in the
          balled brown socks.
In the cold morning car classical radio stations.
In tobacco smoke and pineapple sherbet.
In a bad joke about an armless bell-ringer.
In impossible crossword puzzles.
In cheese sandwiches and diet coke.
In books found and immediately read.
In my grandmother's loneliness and my
          mother's obsession with presidents.
My grandfather is everywhere, in glimpses, and again
in four letters across, meaning "desire or insistence."

Greeley, Nebraska

It's not yet a full day
and my directions are lost.
I imagine the cold of 3 am Nebraska
and Beth, in her overstuffed
orange chair, a beige sweater
knotty and warm and buttonless,
Dink circling at her feet.

But she was in bed,
in a housedress I've probably
never seen, the sweat of morphine sleep
darkening her hair, her daughters
pacing, her husband set
like an uneasy hound
in an overstuffed chair.

For her funeral,
the crowds will circle the Legion Hall,
shuffling slowly and sobbing
down the open streets that
just last year we played in,
when everyone gathered
for her birthday,
when the entire town played tag.

I kept ending up on Beth's porch,
bathed in the smell of hamloaf
and sheet cake, carrying
too-large pineapple salads to picnic tables,
and giggling at her whisper
"quick drink? Come with me."
And I went.

And the town got away from me.

Sunday Afternoon

In this house,
we love like criminals.
We steal time.
Lock the doors,
send the kids
on imaginary errands.

Our clothes are flash paper
turned to smoke.
It only takes
this secret and skin
to skin to remember.

On your hands,
soap and exhaustion.
On mine,
onions and cold cream.

The dogs bark to everyone—
they've been locked out.
Do you know?
The man and the woman,
they've been locked in!

How it makes our mouths
water. How we turn
back into our room
and I am translucent.

You have been tied
with bed sheets
into a sheet bend,
loosened to mooring
hitch by sweat.

The dogs rush in
when we try to escape
for water—
they sniff everything.
They know all
about our crimes.

Trained

The goldfish
has been trained.

He knows
when the light comes on
that we are coming,

swims over
to the side of the bowl
where the orange can
of fish flakes
rests just beyond
the curvature
of glass.

He hovers,
if a fish can be said to hover,
as if to say
mom mom mom mom mom
Hey mom—it's morning and
I'm starving.

And when I pick up
the fish flakes,
crush them with my thumb
onto the water's surface,
he dances a circle
or two and rushes
mouth wide to the top.

But just as often,
I forget to feed him
entirely.

Afterglow

for John Swaile on the day of his wake

It doesn't always end with a bang.
Sometimes it sneaks up on you,
builds quietly until you can hold out
no longer, and seize, exhausted,
skin tingling almost too much to touch.

I roll everything over in my mind.
What you enjoyed, what you tried
to help me with, what I want to do
again, and how you looked at just
that moment when we were together
and even later, when you blushed and
thought I wasn't looking.

I want to say something unbelievable,
something that makes you
laugh from your belly
or stop and hold your breath, or
wipe your brow the way you
always did when you had
something to say. I want you to say
how very very wonderful.

But it is late, and already,
you are asleep.

Jonie **McIntire** is a member of Almeda Street Poets, Toledo Poetry Museum, and can be found at toledopoet.com. She is the Poetry Editor of the *Toledo Streets Newspaper* and coordinator of the annual 100 Thousand Poets for Change events in Toledo. As Treasurer of a place-based 501(c)3 named Sylvania Avenue Neighbors, she works to enhance arts and support for artists in her West Toledo neighborhood.

Her work has been published in the online journal *Red Fez, Sam & Andy's Uptown Café* (Westron Press, 2001), *Broadway Bards First* (The Poetry Barn, 2010), and *Toledo Poetry Project,* Volume 1, Issue 3 (2014). Her poem "Work Night" won 2nd place in the *Toledo City Paper*'s Poetry Contest in 2015. And her poems have even been stamped into cement as part of the Arts Commission of Greater Toledo's Sidewalk Poetry series.

Jonie lives in Toledo, Ohio with her factory-working poet husband, two very active children, two yappy dogs and, occasionally, some goldfish.